FAITH MOVES GOD

FAITH MOVES GOD

Prophetess Debra Reagans

Scripture quotations marked KJV are from the Holy Bible, King James Version (Authorized Version). First published in 1611. Quoted from the KJV Classic Reference Bible, Copyright © 1983 by The Zondervan Corporation.

Scripture taken from The Holy Bible, King James Version. Public Domain

Any people depicted in stock imagery provided by Getty Images are models, and such images are being used for illustrative purposes only.
Certain stock imagery © Getty Images.

Print information available on the last page.

Rev. date: 09/14/2020

To order additional copies of this book, contact:
Xlibris
844-714-8691
www.Xlibris.com
Orders@Xlibris.com
818056

This book is dedicated in memory of my parents, Dallas and Louise Abdalla who taught me to think about others instead of myself. My mom always had a house full of people, whether they needed food, clothes, or a place to stay. She opened our home to everyone. They both made many sacrifices in their life to give us their absolute best. I love and miss you mom and dad.

FAITH MOVES GOD

CONTENTS

FAITH MOVES GOD

ACKNOWLEDGMENTS

I would like to dedicate this book to my Lord and Savior Jesus Christ. To my husband Cedric, my coach and my best friend, I would like to thank you for your love, support, and encouragement. To our children, I want the best for each of you, Love Mom. To our grands, I breathe and live more and more each day when I see the smiles and laughter each of you bring.

To our first great-grandbaby Cam, so full of joy and laughter, we love you. To my brothers and sisters, Mom and Dad instill so much love in us. Always love one another. To Minister Angela Adams, my BFF forever, a powerful prayer warrior who covers me in prayer, thanks for hanging in there with me. Thank you Minister Cheryl Royston for that sister love and the beautiful photos on my book cover. Pastor Randy and Prophetess Mingo, what can I say, thank you for pouring into my life. Thank you Dr. Linda Callaway for pushing me to complete any goal that is set before me. To Apostle Debra Ford, you have instilled so much in me. You believed in me. Thank you! To my co-laborers in the ministry, thank you for your obedience to the Father. Continue to allow Christ to use you to bring souls into the kingdom.

INTRODUCTION

This book will encourage, edify, and inspire you to walk in the gift of faith. Have faith to believe that anything your heart desires, God can provide. FAITH is invisible. The word of the Lord says this in Hebrews 11:1, KJV, *"Now faith is the substance of things hoped for, the evidence of things not seen."* FAITH is unseen in the natural but hoped for in the supernatural. In this book, I will take you through a journey of FAITH that will teach you how to depend on God and only Him. You will rise above all your circumstances and enter into a place of love, peace, and rest with God. We all need FAITH to overcome all challenges in our life. You will learn how to keep moving despite everything happening around you. Endure the sufferings of Christ as a good solider. Let us take this walk of FAITH in God together. Let God be God in your life. I pray that God will increase and multiply your FAITH in Him.

FAITH
MOVES
GOD

CHAPTER 1

Faith in Christ

Jeremiah 1:5 KJV, "Before I formed thee in the belly I knew thee; and before thou camest forth out of the womb I sanctified thee, and I ordained thee a prophet unto the nations.

I remember being in my drama class in the seventh grade. I felt like my teacher was so hard on me. She would drill me and drill me on everything I did. I would find myself crying and upset after her class. The Lord was using her to stir up the gift that was in me. I became an outstanding scholar in drama. She put me in competition after competition. God was building my FAITH in speaking and preparing me for the journey He had for me.

I spoke on a program at school later that year. It so happened to be on Judgment Day by Langston Hughes. Well, guess what, I wore a white robe, and the play was basically talking about God raining down fire. Wow, the entire auditorium was filled with students, teachers, principals, and administrators. They were all standing, clapping, and shouting. This was the very first message God had given me to preach to His people.

Sometime that year, I cannot recall exactly what night it all happened, I decided to go into my parents' bedroom for something, LOL, probably trying to get the phone from under my mother's pillow, which she had hidden. I was stopped suddenly while I was standing at the foot of the bed that night. My parents were sleeping, and they did not awake. A vision appeared before my very eyes. It was a clear image of Jesus Christ stretching out His hands for me. I could see the nails prints in His hands. I was not afraid at all. I felt so much peace, and the presence of Him was indescribable. I stood there gazing and astonished of what I was seeing with my own eyes. I could see into His eyes and felt so much love and compassion. He had His hands still reaching out to me. That was the night it all started; it was my first visitation from God. I wanted to touch Him like Thomas did just to see if He was really Christ.

John 20:26-28 KJV, "And after eight days again his disciples were within, and Thomas with them: then came Jesus, the doors

being shut, and stood in the midst, and said, Peace be unto you.
Then saith he to Thomas, Reach hither thy finger, and behold
my hands; and reach hither thy hand, and thrust it into my side:
and be not faithless, but believing. And Thomas answered and
said unto him, My Lord and my God."

I decided to take my hand to touch Him that same night, and my hand went through the image of Him standing before me. His presence left me at the very moment. I remember going back to bed, and I never told no one what had happen to me that night. People of God, Christ is with us every day of our life. He wants us to communicate with Him so He can reveal mysteries to us. He is waiting for us to spend quality time with Him. Christ has so much He wants to give us. We just need to believe that anything is possible. He sits on the throne, and He is interceding on your behalf. He is calling us to believe that we have a purpose here in the earth for Him. He has given us authority and power to overcome the works of darkness. FAITH is believing in Him and depending on Christ for everything in our life. He holds the key in His hands, and He is giving us the opportunity to use them for our good. I knew that very night that Christ was calling me and preparing me. I believe for such a time as this.

Esther 4:14 KJV, "For if thou altogether holdest thy peace at this time, then shall there enlargement and deliverance arise to the Jews from another place; but thou and thy father's house shall be destroyed: and who knoweth whether thou art come to the kingdom for such a time as this?"

CHAPTER 2

Where Is Your Faith?

James 2:17 KJV, "Even so faith, if it hath not works, is dead, being alone"

This is life . . . People of God, we will go through seasons of pain and seasons of joy.

Isaiah 61:3, KJV, "To appoint unto them that mourn in Zion, to give unto them beauty for ashes, the oil of joy for mourning, the garment of praise for the spirit of heaviness; that they might be called trees of righteousness, the planting of the LORD, that he might be glorified."

This is called the cycle of life. Some of you may be coming out of one or about to enter that season. I found myself back in a place without faith trying to hold on to everything. I could not comprehend the idea of going through this again. I knew God and I still wrestled with myself in and out of different seasons in my life.

I had seasons of great faith and seasons of low slung-down faith. I wanted to tell God no, not right now. I cannot deal with this right now, and I cannot cope with being under this type of pressure any longer. I have gone through enough, and enough is enough. I cannot do this right now. There were times I would tell God I am done, why is this occurring again.

Yes, despite of what was going on in my life, I battled in my spirit, and I knew the word of God. We will all go through seasons of adversities and anguish. But just remember, we are just going, it's not meant for us to stay in that season.

You are not alone, and God has not forgotten about you. He sees all, and He know all. Things are going to get better for you.

I was going through a season when my life was turning upside down. I realize now that God was sending me through a period of breaking. He was preparing me for greater and better things to do. This is where I had to put all my trust in Him for the things I needed.

Proverbs 3:5-6, "Trust in the Lord with all thine heart; and lean not to your understanding. In all your ways acknowledge Him, and He shall direct your paths."

The pressure from God brings the anointing, the power and working of the Holy Spirit. The anointing destroys the yolk of bondage. When the yolk of bondage is broken, your freedom comes.

I adore having conversation with God whether they are terrific or sad. I let Him know exactly how I am feeling and what is on my mind. I can tell God when I am upset and express to Him all my feelings. He would say to me it is going to be well in your soul. God is going to bring you out of this position. He is going to hold your hand and walk with you. "Your FAITH IN GOD WILL INCREASE." He is coming to see about you.

What, really, how is everything going to be alright? Right now, I feel that my life is falling apart and there is nowhere to turn. My faith was spiraling downhill. Instead of depending on God, we give up on Him. I merely was in a place when I did not want to talk to God and did not want to pray.

I certainly did not want to hear a prophetic word about what God is going to do this for me. Be strong in the Lord and power of His might. I was angry, afraid, frustrated, bitter, upset, and had feelings of great doubt.

Jesus told the disciples in *Luke 8:22 KJV, "Now it came to pass on a certain day, that he went into a ship with his disciples: and he said unto them, Let us go over unto the other side of the lake. And they launched forth."*

We can't imagine or even comprehend the things that may happen on the other side. I am sure the disciples were afraid, unsatisfied, and furious that Jesus decided that He would take a nap and go to sleep when they really needed Him.

That is just the way we feel when God does not show up for us when we want Him too. Mary and Martha were pretty upset when they sent for Him and He did not come until Lazarus had already died.

They depended on Him for everything, and He had the audacity not to come when He was called upon. Sounds just like us! He should have been here. He needs to come and resolve this problem I am having or at least show some concerns. He is waiting for us to die to ourselves and our selfish ways, so He can appear on the scene.

Once we learned to move—I, we, they, me, him, and her out the way—then God can move in and take care of the problem. Really, it is not a problem, we just need the word to move and move quick.

It is a daily walk with God. He is always speaking, directing, and guiding us to enter in or cross over into something new. Yes, in that crossing, it may be rough, but He shows up during the midst of a storm.

Matthew 8:26 KJV, "And he saith unto them, Why are ye fearful, O ye of little faith? Then he arose, and rebuked the winds and the sea; and there was a great calm."

I know that things are going to happen in our lifetime, but they are designed from the foundation of the world. It was called into existence then, and it comes into fruition in that season. There is nothing that transpires unless God called it to be. Blank faith is when you have no faith that God will move for you.

You find all kinds of ways to do it yourself. Blank faith is when you cannot see yourself coming out, and you have no idea how it is going to happen. Blank faith is when you depend on yourself, or you put your trust in people instead of God. Blank faith is just blank. You are just empty without God.

You begin to search for freedom in friend, family, and people. You begin to speak words of failure and condemnation over the things you are going through. You call death to the situation in its place instead of calling it back to life. You fight against the power of God and block Him from moving or opening doors to release the blessing into your hands.

You allow the enemy to close doors that God have given you access to use. Blank faith causes the heavens to close. Blank faith opens the door for the enemy to kill, steal, and destroy your spirit. When you walk in blank faith, you will realize it is not about you. It is about the God in you. He wants to awaken the ability in you to believe there is faith in God.

He is the only one who will give you what you need. Blank faith will close your hand to the things of God.

In a season of blank faith, you must find time to read the word, seek the word, listen to the word. Get in a place of worship and pray until you get your breakthrough. Focus on the things of God, be accountable to someone, your pastor, a friend, your spouse, but never give up on God.

CHAPTER 3

Having Faith

Great men and women of God had great FAITH, and they all had to get here at some point. Just think about Christ for a moment. He was led in the wilderness.

Matthew 4:1 KJV, "Then was Jesus led up of the wilderness to be tempted of the devil.

He tempted Jesus in the wilderness during His forty-day journey that was led by the Holy Spirit, but Jesus withstood the test in the midst of His wilderness experience. The enemy will come after you in diverse seasons, it is his agenda for you to fall.

When Jesus came out of the wilderness, His ministry began to blossom in the things of God in a greater volume. He learned to suffer in the things of God with boundless faith. God will show up and show out in your life. Jesus was always busy traveling and serving the nations. He was about His Father's business. He only took time to pray and rest in different seasons.

If we continue to walk in darkness, it cripples the FAITH we have in us.

The enemy really can trap your mind if you let him, but God gives us the power to subdue the works of darkness.

Galatians 5:19-21 KJV, "Now the works of the flesh are manifest, which are these; Adultery, fornication, uncleanness, lasciviousness, Idolatry, witchcraft, hatred, variance, emulations, wrath, strife, seditions, heresies, Envyings, murders, drunkenness, revellings, and such like: of the which I tell you before, as I have also told you in time past, that they which do such things shall not inherit the kingdom of God."

When you are in a truncated state, you will find yourself caught up in a dark place. In a dark place, the things of God are shut off from you, and the enemy will have havoc with your life. The Holy Spirit is our helper, and He will come in and bring you out of the state of confusion, depressions, sickness, and disease. God wants to use you for His glory. The works of the flesh are cast out, and the gifts of the spirit began to operate in you. There is a greater purpose for your life.

The glory of God can only be revealed and disclosed with FAITH in God. Having FAITH in God can take you over to the other side.

Elijah was running for his life, hiding from the things of God.

1 Kings 19:4-5 KJV, *"But he himself went a day's journey into the wilderness, and came and sat down under a juniper tree: and he requested for himself that he might die; and said, It is enough; now, O LORD, take away my life; for I am not better than my fathers. And as he lay and slept under a juniper tree, behold, then an angel touched him, and said unto him, Arise and eat.*

He finds himself depressed, angry, tired of life, and wanted to give up. He told God he was fed up and wanted to die, but God had more for him to do. The Lord was strengthening and preparing him for his next assignment. The angel of the Lord shows up twice to give him food and water. God just wants us to trust in Him.

1 Kings 19:6-9 KJV, "And he looked, and, behold, there was a cake baken on the coals, and a cruse of water at his head. And he did eat and drink, and laid him down again. And the angel of the LORD came again the second time, and touched him, and said, Arise and eat; because the journey is too great for thee. And he arose, and did eat and drink, and went in the strength of that meat forty days and forty nights unto Horeb the mount of God. And he came thither unto a cave, and lodged there; and, behold, the word of the LORD came to him, and he said unto him, What doest thou here, Elijah?"

We can get stuck sometimes, and we cannot find a way of escape. God suddenly shows up on time to help us get back up again. Elijah was led right back into the things of God to complete his God-given assignment.

We have all been in a season where the enemy has tormented our mind. I found myself in a low state, a place called Lo-Debar. This was a dry place where my hope was gone, and I could not find a way out. I had to learned how to trust in God. My faith was tested time and time again. God will send someone to bless you. He always has a ram in the bush waiting just for you. Sometimes we cannot find our way out of a hard place, but He shows up on the scene just in time. When we learn to have FAITH in God, He will move in ways you could never imagine. He will show up in a supernatural way.

2 Samuel 9:1-7 KJV, "And David said, Is there yet any that is left of the house of Saul, that I may shew him kindness for Jonathan's sake? And there was of the house of Saul a servant whose name was Ziba. And when they had called him unto David, the king said unto him, Art thou Ziba? And he said, Thy servant is he. And the king said, Is there not yet any of the house of Saul, that I may shew the kindness of God unto him? And Ziba said unto the king, Jonathan hath yet a son, which is lame on his feet. And the king said unto him, Where is he? And Ziba said unto the king, Behold, he is in the house of Machir, the son of Ammiel, in Lodebar. Then king David sent, and fetched him out of the house of Machir, the son of Ammiel, from Lodebar. Now when Mephibosheth, the son of Jonathan, the son of Saul, was come unto David, he fell on his face, and did reverence. And David said, Mephibosheth. And he answered, Behold thy servant! And David said unto him, Fear not: for I will surely shew thee kindness for Jonathan thy father's sake, and will restore thee all the land of Saul thy father; and thou shalt eat bread at my table continually."

When you find yourself in that place, if you cannot do anything else, just call on the name of the Lord, and He will answer you and do great and mighty things. God always has someone working behind the scenes to come and bless you.

King David wanted to show his kindness and bless Saul's household. He took Jonathan's son from that low state he was in and took him to that kingdom place and fed him the things of God to encourage him, to build him up, and to give him the goods of the land. Everything he ever desired was given to him to prosper and to inherit the kingdom of God.

He was blessed above measure and did not want for anything. He had entered a new season called there, a season of reaping the blessing from God. God never leaves us, and He will never forsake us. He is always standing guard over our life. When the roadblocks come, they are only there for a reason and a season.

We learn how to accept the things we cannot change. The enemy will come to steal your joy to keep you from prospering in the things of God. Learn to press through the adversity and watch God begin to create miracles for you.

Matthew 17:20 KJV, "And Jesus said unto them, Because of your unbelief: for verily I say unto you, If ye have faith as a grain of mustard seed, ye shall say unto this mountain, Remove hence to yonder place; and it shall remove; and nothing shall be impossible unto you."

If you have a mustard seed of FAITH, God can still create miracles in your life. You have the power to speak to any circumstance in your life that brings you sorrow. God can turn your sorrow into joy.

Your joy and strength come from above. God is the only one who can change your situation if you let Him. We always want to stick our hands in everything instead of taking it to God. We must believe and have faith so He can demonstrate His power and love for us.

FAITH MOVES GOD

CHAPTER 4

Now Faith

Hebrews 11:6 KJV, "Now faith is the substance of things hoped for, the evidence of things not seen.

I have read this scripture multiple times and still find myself struggling with the big word called faith. We must remind ourselves that without faith at all, it is impossible for God to move. Faith is an action word; it is a word of movement. God wants to move for you. Do not act like Abraham and Sarah.

They both took things into their own hands to help fulfill the promise that God spoke over their lives. He told him at his old age that him and Sarah would have a son.

Genesis 18:12 KJV, "Therefore Sarah laughed within herself, saying, After I am waxed old shall I have pleasure, my lord being old also?"

When it did not happen fast enough, Sarah gave him this great idea to sleep with her handmaiden. We are always trying to put our hands in our situation. The Lord has already said I am going to handle it for you.

We need to learn how to be still so God can move. Some of us are so hardheaded, we continue to take the test repeatedly. When I was in school, I wanted to pass my test every time. I did not want to repeat it. I wanted to move on to the next grade level. God is trying to take us to another dimension in the spirit, but without faith, it is hard to please Him.

Let God be God in your life so He can move you to that next dimension in Him. God has so much more for you, but you must remove your hands and allow Him to move. God wants to open doors for you according to *Revelation 3:8 KJV, "I know thy works: behold, I have set before thee an open door, and no man can shut it: for thou hast a little strength, and hast kept my word, and hast not denied my name."*

You must believe in yourself. You can choose to speak life or death over your situation. Choose life every morning your feet touch the floor. There is so much power and authority in you.

You just need to believe and trust God to do the rest. You are here to worship and praise the Lord with your whole heart. Give God all of you and watch how He began to change you and your situation.

Life can be hard if you let it, but it you give it all to God, it will be so much easier. Let God be God in your life. We are going to have setbacks in our life, but when it is over, God has something greater for you to do.

1 John 4:4 KJV, "Ye are of God, little children, and have overcome them: because greater is he that is in you, than he that is in the world."

God is not done with you; it is not over. It has just started, and it is marvelous in His sight.

Think about the word "impossible." Webster defines it as incapable of being or of occurring to, be incapable of being done, attained, or fulfilled.

Mark 9:23 KJV, "Jesus said unto him, If thou canst believe, all things are possible to him that believeth."

You are capable, you can do whatever you want. You just need the faith of God, and He will lead and guide you.

He has already called you to do it, just trust Him. You were formed in your mother's womb for a purpose, and that purpose is to serve the Almighty.

He knew you would have a lack of faith. That is why He only required you to at least have mustard-seed faith. That kind of faith would move mountains. I have seen God show up in my life at the very last minute. He would always be right on time. He never let me down.

Psalms 37:25, "I have been young, and now am old; yet have I not seen the righteous forsaken, nor his seed begging for bread."

CHAPTER 5

Walking in Faith

2 Corinthians 5:7, "For we walk by faith, not by sight."

I decided to take a leap of FAITH in God. I decided to step out of myself and allow God to use me for His glory. God was waiting for me to move myself out of the way so He could be glorified. I had to do a lot of fasting and praying to get to this moment in my life.

I just wanted to sit on the back burner and watch everyone else on fire for God. I decided to stop walking in fear. My FAITH began to increase in God. I realized that God did not put me here to just sit but to worship and praise His name. The enemies' target is to breakdown your faith. He knows if we live by faith, it is our lifeline to the Father. When you begin to draw closer to God, His word will work miracles for you. Faith cannot be seen because it is invisible. Faith comes from waiting on God's presence, seeking His face so we can hear His voice.

The Lord has given us all a level of faith. He increases our faith the more we spend time in the word and prayer. The more we commune with Him, fear disappears, and we begin to excel in our faith. God has given us so many gifts, and they are dormant. He wants you to have the faith to believe. We all have the anointing of God to walk by faith.

2 Corinthians 5:7, "For we walk by faith, not by sight."

Let God take you to that secret place so He can speak mysteries to you. He wants you to take that leap of FAITH so He can bless you. Faith will take you to places you have not seen. Faith will take you into open doors you could not enter. Faith will give you favor with God and with man.

Faith will take you into the deep things of God. Faith will open your eyes and ears into the spiritual realm. Faith will increase and multiply you. The mysteries of God will be revealed to you at a deeper measure in the spirit.

2 Timothy 1:7 KJV, "For God hath not given us the spirit of fear; but of power, and of love, and of a sound mind."

Leave fear and enter FAITH and allow God to use you. It is so much in you that God wants to pour out of you.

John 7:38 "He that believeth on me, as the scripture hath said, out of his belly shall flow rivers of living water."

FAITH
MOVES
GOD

CHAPTER 6

The Gifts of Faith

1 Corinthians 12:7-11 KJV, *"But the manifestation of the Spirit is given to every man to profit withal. For to one is given by the Spirit the word of wisdom; to another the word of knowledge by the same Spirit; To another faith by the same Spirit; to another the gifts of healing by the same Spirit; To another the working of miracles; to another prophecy; to another discerning of spirits; to another divers kinds of tongues; to another the interpretation of tongues: But all these worketh that one and the selfsame Spirit, dividing to every man severally as he will."*

Allow the Holy Spirit to manifest these power gifts in your life. Let God use the gifts in you to bless others. You just must believe in God and have FAITH. All you need is a mustard seed! I pray that God will give you the gift of FAITH to do miracles, signs, and wonders.

Mark 16:15-20 KJV, "And he said unto them, Go ye into all the world, and preach the gospel to every creature. He that believeth and is baptized shall be saved; but he that believeth not shall be damned. And these signs shall follow them that believe; In my name shall they cast out devils; they shall speak with new tongues; They shall take up serpents; and if they drink any deadly thing, it shall not hurt them; they shall lay hands on the sick, and they shall recover. So then after the Lord had spoken unto them, he was received up into heaven, and sat on the right hand of God. And they went forth, and preached every where, the Lord working with them, and confirming the word with signs following. Amen."

1. The Word of Knowledge . . . Supernatural knowledge that comes directly from the Holy Spirit.
2. The Word of Wisdom . . . Supernatural ability to apply the wisdom the Holy Spirit has given you.
3. The Gift of Prophecy . . . Supernatural word from The Lord.
4. The Gift of Faith . . . Supernatural sense in your mind and spirit that will cause you to believe in faith.
5. The Gifts of Healings . . . Supernatural power of the Holy Spirit can manifest this gift to the believer to heal someone.
6. The Working of Miracles . . . Supernatural acts of God.
7. The Discerning of Spirits . . . Supernatural insight.

8. Different Kinds of Tongues . . . Supernatural ability to speak on a foreign tongue.

9. The Interpretation of Tongues . . . Supernatural ability to understand.

What is the supernatural? It is that thing that cannot not be explained by the natural eye. It is all supernatural! Why? Because it is all God Himself. He has all power in his hand.

Acts 1:8, "But you will receive power, after that the Holy Spirit is come upon you; and ye shall be witnesses unto me both in Jerusalem, and in all Judea and Samaria, and unto the uttermost part of the earth."

He rules, and He reigns. He is Alpha and Omega. He is the beginning and the end. When you walk in faith, the power of God will take control of your life, and you will see the glory of God released in your life.

Take that step of faith and run with the gift and never look back at fear. Fear has no power in your life. If you are reading this right now, at this very moment, I decree and declare that your FAITH is blooming now in the name of Jesus. I prophesy that you have entered another dimension in the spirit. God is going to use you for His glory. People of God, you must believe in the impossible if you can just believe. I have learned over the years to take one day at a time. This is a statement I live by every day.

Matthew 6:25 KJV, "Therefore I say unto you, Take no thought for your life, what ye shall eat, or what ye shall drink; nor yet for your body, what ye shall put on. Is not the life more than meat, and the body than raiment? Behold the fowls of the air: for they sow not, neither do they reap, nor gather into barns; yet your heavenly Father feedeth them. Are ye not much better than they?"

We must learn how to depend on God to sustain us from day to day. That is FAITH in God. He sustained the prophet Elijah and the widow at Zarephath.

1 King 17:9-16 KJV, "A rise, get thee to Zarephath, which belongeth to Zidon, and dwell there: behold, I have commanded a widow woman there to sustain thee. So he arose and went to Zarephath. And when he came to the gate of the city, behold, the widow woman was there gathering of sticks: and he called to her, and said, Fetch me, I pray thee, a little water in a vessel, that I may drink. And as she was going to fetch it, he called to her, and said, Bring me, I pray thee, a morsel of bread in thine hand. And she said, As the LORD thy God liveth, I have not a cake, but an handful of meal in a barrel, and a little oil in a cruse: and, behold, I am gathering two sticks, that I may go in and dress it for me and my son, that we may eat it, and die. And Elijah said unto her, Fear not; go and do as thou hast said: but make me thereof a little cake first, and bring it unto me, and after make for thee and for thy son. For thus saith the LORD God of Israel, The barrel of meal shall not waste, neither shall the cruse of oil fail, until the day that the LORD sendeth rain upon the earth. And she went and did according to the saying of Elijah: and she, and he, and her house, did eat many days. And the barrel of meal wasted not, neither did the cruse of oil fail, according to the word of the LORD, which he spake by Elijah."

He sustained the children of Israel in the wilderness.

Exodus 16:35, "And the children of Israel did eat manna forty years, until they came to a land inhabited; they did eat manna, until they came unto the borders of the land of Canaan."

We must believe God for everything that we need. He knows what we need, and He wants to bless us each day. He wants to bless His children and gives us hidden treasures. He is our source, our provider.

Let God be God in your life! God loves you! He wants what best for you!

FAITH
MOVES
GOD

CHAPTER 7

Faith in God

This has been a faith walk for me. I did not begin to understand what faith really meant until I received the call of God. I begin to understand faith more and more each day. Faith became my entire life. I had to live and walk by faith. Nothing came easy for me. I had to work hard for everything I needed. I could not understand at times why life had to be so hard. Life becomes hard without faith.

Life will make you search yourself for everything. I had to find out what was missing in my life and what God was trying to make me see. I finally realized that I could not depend on man for anything. God wanted me to totally depend on Him. I was depending on everybody else but God. When I look back over my life, I know that God was there all along. I just did not have the faith to believe. Faith is powerful, and you just need a mustard seed of that to believe.

Debra had FAITH in God for herself. God was building my Faith in Him. I would stay in my bedroom for days fasting, praying, and reading the word of God. I had so many experiences with God in my home. I had dreams night after night that would occur. I had visions of me standing in my kitchen and rain was falling all around me and it never touched me. I had visions of being in caught up in a whirlwind. God was building my FAITH in Him. I had outer body experiences where I could see my spirit leave my body. I could feel the wind of God so strong in my bedroom it would turn the pages of any book I was reading.

One day I had a vision of the images of Christ, Peter, James, and John. My backdoor open and they walk in. Jesus was in the front and the disciples in the back with fish on a fishing pole. I heard the Lord say to me follow me. I will make you fisherman of men. They walked through my house from the backdoor and exited out the front door.

The Lord was building my Faith and the enemy would try and come in from time to time and distract me. I was home one morning alone laying on the couch in my living room. I started smelling a foul odor in the room. I felt his nasty presence and suddenly the enemy came from behind me and began to breath in my ear. I reached over my head to grab him and I could feel his nasty hair and body. See, the devil shows up from time to time to try and stop your destiny in God. He has no power to stop what God will do in your life.

You must have FAITH in God and BELIEVE. I begin to plead the blood of Jesus over my life and he disappeared that very instant. God continued to show me miracles, signs, and wonders to build my FAITH in Him. The Lord would tell me if someone was sick. I could walk in a hospital room and would know if someone was going to live or die. I could smell death when I would enter a room. God would show me dreams when someone I knew was going to die. He came to me one night and told me He was bringing my dad home. I remember asking God not to take him now, but God said it was his time. He told me about one of my brothers and one of my sisters. He showed me walking one of my sisters through a tunnel and when we got to the other side it was beautiful flowers everywhere. She was smiling at me waving goodbye. I could not say anything because no one would believe that God was speaking to me.

I have had so many experiences with God I cannot tell them all. I remember calling our Pastor asking her to pray for me. I was overwhelmed with the things God was showing and telling me. I understand now that He had to strengthen me and build my FAITH. He wanted to use me to bring souls into the Kingdom. I had to feel pain and joy in my walk with God. I had to have the FAITH to tell them that God is with you and He will never leave you or forsake you. I know God is real and He will be right there with you.

God is going to build your FAITH in Him. God was trusting me with so much. My FAITH in Him increased more and more each day. People will never understand you and the anointing of God upon your life. It is something they will have to experience for themselves. I will continue to allow God to use me for His glory to bring souls into the Kingdom.

Moses had to stand before the pharaoh and demand he let God's people go. He could have gotten killed, but he knew God was his deliverer.

Noah, who obeyed God, built the ark.

Abraham, the father of faith, was told by God told to leave his country and start a new nation.

Hannah, barren for years, believed God and gave birth to Samuel the prophet.

Esther stood before the king to save the Jews.

Mary, whom the angel appeared to, was told that she would carry the Christ.

FAITH! Hidden Treasures

Hebrews 11:4 KJV, "By faith Abel offered unto God a more excellent sacrifice than Cain, by which he obtained witness that he was righteous, God testifying of his gifts: and by it he being dead yet speaketh."

Hebrews 11:5 KJV, "By faith Enoch was translated that he should not see death; and was not found, because God had translated him: for before his translation he had this testimony, that he pleased God."

Scriptures on FAITH! Some Gems from the Word of God

Numbers 14:24 KJV, "But my servant Caleb, because he had another spirit with him, and hath followed me fully, him will I bring into the land whereinto he went; and his seed shall possess it."

Psalm 9:10 KJV, "And they that know thy name will put their trust in thee: for thou, LORD, hast not forsaken them that seek thee.

FAITH
MOVES
GOD

CHAPTER 8

Faith Nuggets

I use them daily. They keep my spirit grounded and rooted in the word of God.

Psalm 1:3, "And he shall be like a tree planted by the rivers of water, that bringeth forth his fruit in his season; his leaf also shall not wither; and whatsoever he doeth shall prosper."

1. Good morning, Holy Spirit! Speak to Him every morning.
2. Prayer - Communicate with God.
3. Adoration - Acknowledge God in everything you do.
4. Praise - Worship God.
5. Thanksgiving - Thank God for the things He do.

Questions to think on

1. What is FAITH?
2. How much FAITH do I need to depend on God?
3. Can I trust God with my life?
4. Will God answer me in my time of need?
5. Can He deliver me from sickness and disease?
6. What about my love ones?

Let Us Pray

Father God, I acknowledge who You are today, I bless Your Holy name. Holy Spirit, lead and guide me, instill in me a greater level of FAITH. Jesus, give me the FAITH I need to believe and trust in Your word. God, thank You for leading and guiding me alone the way. I believe that my FAITH will increase as I stay before Your face in prayer. I will commune with You, Lord, each day of my life. Thank You, Lord, for the faith that You have given me to move mountains. I believe it, and I receive it. In JESUS's NAME, I PRAY, AMEN AND AMEN.

Be encouraged, people of God! The Father wants to use you!

FAITH MOVES GOD

Some things to Journal about your Faith walk

1. Faith is love taking the form of aspirations------William Ellery Channing

What is Faith to you?

_____

_____

_____

_____

_____

_____

_____

_____

_____

_____

_____

_____

_____

_____

_____

_____

_____

FAITH MOVES GOD

Some things to Journal about your Faith walk

2. Faith, as an intellectual state, is self-reliance------O.W. Holmes

Is Faith self-reliance?

_____
_____
_____
_____
_____
_____
_____
_____
_____
_____
_____
_____
_____
_____
_____
_____
_____
_____

FAITH MOVES GOD

Some things to Journal about your Faith walk

3. Faith is the force of life-----Leo Tolstoy

Faith forces us to keep going

_____

_____

_____

_____

_____

_____

_____

_____

_____

_____

_____

_____

_____

_____

_____

_____

_____

_____

FAITH MOVES GOD

Some things to Journal about your Faith walk

4. Give to Faith the things that belong to Faith-----Bacon, Advancement of Learning

Faith belongs to you

_____

_____

_____

_____

_____

_____

_____

_____

_____

_____

_____

_____

_____

_____

FAITH MOVES GOD

Some things to Journal about your Faith walk

5. You can do very little with Faith, but you can do nothing without it-------Samuel Butler

You can do nothing without Faith

_____

_____

_____

_____

_____

_____

_____

_____

_____

_____

_____

_____

_____

_____

_____

_____

_____

FAITH MOVES GOD

Some things to Journal about your Faith walk

6. Faith needs her daily bread------Dinah M.M.Craik

We need Faith daily

_____

_____

_____

_____

_____

_____

_____

_____

_____

_____

_____

_____

_____

_____

_____

_____

FAITH MOVES GOD

Some things to Journal about your Faith walk

7. Our Faith triumphant o'er our fears----Longfellow, the building of a ship

We cannot allow fear to control us

FAITH MOVES GOD

Some things to Journal about your Faith walk

8. A perfect Faith would lift us absolutely above fear-----
George Macdonald

You have perfect Faith

_____

_____

_____

_____

_____

_____

_____

_____

_____

_____

_____

_____

_____

_____

_____

FAITH MOVES GOD

Some things to Journal about your Faith walk

9. Ye whose hearts are fresh and simple, who have Faith in God and nature----Longfellow, Hiawatha

Have Faith in God

_____

_____

_____

_____

_____

_____

_____

_____

_____

_____

_____

_____

_____

_____

_____

_____

_____

_____

_____

FAITH MOVES GOD

Some things to Journal about your Faith walk

10. And cling to Faith beyond the forms of Faith---Tennyson

Cling to Faith

_____

_____

_____

_____

_____

_____

_____

_____

_____

_____

_____

_____

_____

_____

_____

_____

FAITH MOVES GOD

Some things to Journal about your Faith walk

11. And all but their Faith was overthrown----William Wetmore

I held on to my Faith

_____

_____

_____

_____

_____

_____

_____

_____

_____

_____

_____

_____

_____

_____

_____

_____

_____

_____

_____

FAITH MOVES GOD

Some things to Journal about your Faith walk

12. Beautiful Faith, surrendering unto time-----Stephen Phillips

Surrender to Faith

FAITH MOVES GOD

Some things to Journal about your Faith walk

13. The way to see by Faith is to shut the eye of reason-----
Benjamin Franklin

Close your eyes of reasoning

_____

_____

_____

_____

_____

_____

_____

_____

_____

_____

_____

_____

_____

_____

_____

FAITH MOVES GOD

Some things to Journal about your Faith walk

14. Reason saw no, till Faith sprung the light------Drygen, Religio Laici

Faith will spring up in you like a light

_____

_____

_____

_____

_____

_____

_____

_____

_____

_____

_____

_____

_____

_____

_____

_____

_____

_____

FAITH MOVES GOD

Some things to Journal about your Faith walk

15. Reason is the triumph of the intellect, faith of the heart---James Schouler

Faith shall always be in your heart

_____

_____

_____

_____

_____

_____

_____

_____

_____

_____

_____

_____

_____

_____

_____

_____

_____

_____

FAITH MOVES GOD

Some things to Journal about your Faith walk

16. Faith without works is nothing worth, as dead as a door-nail unless deeds follow---Langland, Piers Plowman

Faith doesn't work unless you believe

_____

_____

_____

_____

_____

_____

_____

_____

_____

_____

_____

_____

_____

_____

_____

_____

_____

FAITH MOVES GOD

Some things to Journal about your Faith walk

17. Faith is the root of works. A root that produceth nothing is dead----Bishop Thomas Wilson

You must continue to produce works

_____

_____

_____

_____

_____

_____

_____

_____

_____

_____

_____

_____

_____

_____

_____

_____

_____

_____

_____

FAITH MOVES GOD

Some things to Journal about your Faith walk

18. What Faith is there in the faithless----Theognis, Sententice

You cannot be faithless

_____

_____

_____

_____

_____

_____

_____

_____

_____

_____

_____

_____

_____

_____

_____

_____

_____

_____

FAITH MOVES GOD

Some things to Journal about your Faith walk

19. And wisdom cries, I know not anything and only Faith beholds that all is well----S.R.Lysaght

Faith beholds all that is well in our soul

_____

_____

_____

_____

_____

_____

_____

_____

_____

_____

_____

_____

_____

_____

_____

_____

_____

_____

_____

FAITH MOVES GOD

Some things to Journal about your Faith walk

20. He has lost his Faith, what has he left to live on---Pubilius Syrus

You cannot lose Faith in God

_____

_____

_____

_____

_____

_____

_____

_____

_____

_____

_____

_____

_____

_____

_____

_____

_____

_____

FAITH MOVES GOD

Some things to Journal about your Faith walk

21. Faith is holding on to everything I believe ----Prophetess Reagans

Hold on to your Faith

_____

_____

_____

_____

_____

_____

_____

_____

_____

_____

_____

_____

_____

_____

_____

_____

FAITH MOVES GOD

Some things to Journal about your Faith walk

22. Faith can be seen supernaturally----Prophetess Reagans

You cannot see it in the natural

_____

_____

_____

_____

_____

_____

_____

_____

_____

_____

_____

_____

_____

_____

_____

FAITH MOVES GOD

Some things to Journal about your Faith walk

23. Faith is taking one day at a time----Prophetess Reagans

Take one day at a time

_____

_____

_____

_____

_____

_____

_____

_____

_____

_____

_____

_____

_____

_____

_____

_____

_____

_____

NOTES

NOTES

NOTES

FAITH MOVES GOD

CPSIA information can be obtained
at www.ICGtesting.com
Printed in the USA
BVHW030021141020
590973BV00001B/71